SELF-CARE IS SCRIPTURAL

A WORKBOOK to REFRESH YOUR MIND, BODY & SOUL

Teresa Pressley, LMFT
and Teriz Michael, LCSW

AMEN

AMEN Editions
an imprint of Andrews McMeel Publishing
a division of Andrews McMeel Universal

www.andrewsmcmeel.com

25 26 27 28 29 RLP 10 9 8 7 6 5 4 3 2 1

ISBN: 978-1-5248-9507-5

Editor: Jennifer Leight
Designer: Melissa Gerber
Interior Production: Twozdai Hulse
Production Manager: Tamara Haus

Interior illustrations used under license from Shutterstock

FSC www.fsc.org
MIX
Paper | Supporting responsible forestry
FSC® C102842

Andrews McMeel Publishing is committed to the responsible use of natural resources and is dedicated to understanding, measuring, and reducing the impact of our products on the natural world. By choosing this product, you are supporting responsible management of the world's forests. The FSC® label means that the materials used for this product come from well-managed FSC®-certified forests, recycled materials, and other controlled sources.

CONTENTS

INTRODUCTION 5

Believe God's Love for You 9

See the Possibilities 17

Honor Your Calling 25

Be Blessed by Sabbath 33

Find Restoration in Nature 41

Embrace Freedom in Release 49

Hold Space for Discovery 57

Appreciate Your Body 65

Tap into Creativity 73

Connect with Your People 81

Ask for What You Need 91

Quiet Your Soul 99

Welcome Comfort 105

Sleep in God's Peace 111

Trust God's Dreams 117

Seek and Celebrate Joy 125

Give Yourself Grace 133

ABOUT THE AUTHORS 142

"Love your neighbor as yourself."

—MATTHEW 22:39 (NIV)

INTRODUCTION

TAKE A FEW QUIET MOMENTS TO MAKE A LIST of the people, groups, causes, and organizations (such as businesses, schools, and churches) in your life that you care for in some way. Who needs your time, energy, and attention on a regular basis?

Now, here's the million-dollar question: Did you put yourself on the list? If you left yourself out, you're not alone. In our combined three decades of counseling a variety of clients, we've found that most people gloss right over themselves. We tend to neglect that "as yourself" part of Matthew 22:39. But God is working right now to make sure you put yourself on that list—to begin giving yourself the care you deserve as His beloved child.

If you have picked up this workbook, chances are you are a giver. Givers are always looking out for and serving others. That's not a bad thing . . . until we lose ourselves in the effort. Finding a balance between giving to others and taking what you need to care for yourself well can be challenging when you are others-focused. People often say they feel selfish, guilty, and ashamed for thinking about their own needs. But here's the truth: Choosing to care for yourself is scriptural, and it pleases God.

Making room for yourself may take some time and practice (and a lot of prayer!), but God wants to guide you all the way. The exercises in this workbook are designed to help you take the first steps in putting your name on your list. Our hope is that you'll see that caring for both others and yourself is not an either/or choice but a both/and blessing that God has bestowed upon us. It's a declaration of the love and grace God extends to all His creation—including you.

You may have tried self-care practices before that didn't stick. Or you may have been misled to believe that self-care is just worldly whimsy—bubble baths and eye masks. This workbook is grounded in the belief that caring for yourself isn't just about feeling better or checking off a self-care to-do list—it's about aligning your thoughts, actions, and heart with God's Kingdom.

Our world encourages us to look outward, focusing on achievements, appearances, and external circumstances. But God calls us to look upward, fixing our gaze on Him. Self-care from a Christian perspective begins with believing that you are worthy of love—God's love, and your own. The process may feel unfamiliar or even challenging at times, but God is with you every step of the way. As you work through the reflections and exercises in this book, you'll discover that taking time to care for yourself isn't selfish—it's a way of honoring the life God has given you. It's about recognizing that, as His beloved child, you deserve rest, joy, and healing.

You're invited to embark on this journey of self-care, trusting that God will meet you where you are. As you move through this workbook, may you feel the presence of His love, His peace, and His abundant grace in every step. God is not just leading you to care for yourself—He's helping you draw closer to Him in the process.

GUIDELINES FOR GETTING STARTED

Pace yourself: This workbook features seventeen units focused on self-care topics and strategies. Each unit begins with an opening reflection and includes three to five exercises to help you practice self-care in a God-honoring way. It may be helpful to try taking on one unit per week, starting with the reflection on day one and completing exercises throughout the remaining days. But always honor your personal rhythm and let God guide your journey.

Begin with prayer: Each time you sit down to engage with the workbook, begin by asking God to open your heart and mind to wherever He wants to lead you. Invite Him into the process and trust that He is working in your life as you seek His presence.

Consider community: Though this workbook is deeply personal, there's great value in walking through it with others. You might want to start the workbook at the same time as a friend, or even in a small group setting. Sharing your journey with others can provide encouragement, accountability, and insight. Choose how much or how little you share, but know that connection can deepen the experience.

Listen for guidance: As you work through these exercises, pay attention to the whispers of God's guidance. He may prompt you to seek additional support from a pastor, therapist, or counselor. This workbook is not a replacement for professional help, but a complement to the healing and care that God wants to offer you. Remember, God provides us with resources and community so that we don't have to walk the journey alone.

Think about the things of heaven, not the things of earth.

—COLOSSIANS 3:2 (NLT)

BELIEVE GOD'S LOVE FOR YOU

WE CAN SEE OURSELVES AND OUR LIVES THROUGH TWO VIEWS: an earthly lens and a Kingdom lens. Our paths in how we treat ourselves will flow from that choice. When our attention is fixed on what is around us (that earthly perspective) instead of oriented to Who is above us (the Kingdom view), we will always feel disappointed, distracted, and down on how we measure up. We won't believe we deserve the care and love we most certainly do. And that's a tough cycle to break once we enter it.

Even if you push through to give your needs a little attention one day, it won't stick as an ongoing commitment because you're skipping the first crucial and Christ-centered step. We know from cognitive behavioral therapy (what you may see referred to as CBT) that changing thoughts leads to a changed life. We are what we think, and our mind dictates our emotions, behaviors, and responses. So, any first steps toward self-care and self-love begin with sorting out what's supportive and God-sent in our thoughts about ourselves and what are voices from a world that is wearing and tearing us down. The exercises in this unit are designed to help shift your focus from negative thoughts to a more positive and affirming self-view based on an understanding of God's love and presence in your life. You'll use principles from CBT to encourage healthy thought patterns.

1

LET GO OF LABELS

Finally, brothers and sisters, whatever is true, whatever is noble, whatever is right, whatever is pure, whatever is lovely, whatever is admirable—if anything is excellent or praiseworthy—think about such things.

—Philippians 4:8 (NIV)

THE WORLD HAS A WAY OF TRYING TO TELL US WHO WE ARE and what we're worth, but it's not accurate. What disheartening names have you been called in your lifetime? Write them in the space below. Don't hold back.

Now, go back and scribble them out defiantly. Release any hold those destructive labels have on your thoughts and how you treat yourself. You've just made space for God's truth and care to enter in.

2

CLAIM YOUR TRUE CITIZENSHIP

The truth: You are fearfully and wonderfully created by a God who had good thoughts toward you before your conception. Intentionally shift your attention to and ponder your heavenly Father's love for you. Set your mind on Christ and the ways of His Kingdom, where you belong. What feelings do you sense God has toward His children (of which you are a beloved one!)? What does Scripture tell us about His love and grace? (Need some places to start? Try Psalm 139:13–14, Zephaniah 3:17, Romans 5:8, Romans 8:38–39, 1 John 3:1, and 1 John 4:19.)

3

FOCUS ON BLESSINGS

TAKE A MOMENT TO REFLECT ON THREE SPECIFIC THINGS you are grateful for that demonstrate God's love for you. These can be small or large, from a kind word from a friend to a beautiful sunrise. For each blessing, note how it reflects God's care for you and what He wants for you.

1. ______________________________

2. ______________________________

3. ______________________________

4

PERSONALIZE GOD'S PROMISES

Select one Scripture verse that speaks to God's love for you. Rewrite the verse in your own words, applying it directly to your life and circumstances. Then consider how this verse can help you more clearly see God's presence and guidance to care for yourself in your daily experiences.

Example Entry:

Verse:

Jeremiah 31:3b (NIV) "I have loved you with an everlasting love; I have drawn you with unfailing kindness."

Your Version:

"God's love for me is eternal, never fading, and He continually surrounds me with kindness."

Reflection:

"When wrestling with doubts or feelings of unworthiness, I can remember that God's love is constant and unchanging. This truth reassures me of my significance in His eyes and His desire for me to be kind with myself."

Verse:

Your Version:

Reflection:

Do not conform to the pattern of this world, but be transformed by the renewing of your mind.

—ROMANS 12:2A (NIV)

SEE THE POSSIBILITIES

EVEN ONCE WE EMBRACE THE TRUTH THAT WE ARE WORTHY OF SELF-CARE, a sneaky thought from the enemy often follows: *I don't have enough time for self-care!* But if God created day and night and the hours within them, surely He has given us the time we need. The question becomes: How do we choose to see our minutes and use them?

We can get so overwhelmed with our schedules that we become distracted and disheartened. It's not all bad blocks in those schedules, either—we may have great things buried in our days that we simply can't grasp because we're still trying to hold on to control of everything that we can't control. Picture that classic *I Love Lucy* episode in which Lucy and Ethel try to keep up with the endless chocolate appearing on the conveyor belt. Where is the button to slow everything down so we can savor life?

Sure, we chuckle at the comedy of that scene. But distraction can do much greater damage in our lives. It can take our eyes off what we truly need—rest, care, connection, and, most of all, God. To get off that conveyor belt, we need to align our priorities with God's principles, one step at a time. The world tells us to do more, get more, and be more, but God's truth frees us from that. When we hold our God-given identity in our heads and our hearts, we build a new foundation on love—for God, ourselves, and others—rather than a never-ending to-do list. Let's reclaim the goodness of God's time.

1

THE POWER OF FOUR

The default catchall to-do list may look impressive to the world, but it does nothing to help you prioritize and manage your time. Try this instead: Fold a piece of paper in half, then in half again to create four sections. Label them "Important and Urgent," "Important but Not Urgent," "Urgent but Not Important," and "Not Important and Not Urgent." Take a moment to honestly fill in your activities and responsibilities for the week. Then, notice where your time and attention often go.

HOW MUCH IMMEDIATE AND UNDIVIDED ATTENTION often goes to "not important and not urgent" things that induce panic or stretch you thin to complete tasks that are important and urgent?

DO YOU SEE ANYTHING YOU CAN DELEGATE to others to free up time and energy for things only you can do? (Remember, delegating can give others the chance to use their God-given talents too!)

2

REFINE YOUR FOCUS

Imagine you are the cinematographer of your life. What scenes in your day-to-day deserve to be zoomed in on? What's blurred that should come into clearer focus? And what in the background is distracting? Sketch or write your answers, then reflect on what comes to light.

3

BETTER BOUNDARIES

OUR EFFICACY AND EFFICIENCY DEPEND on our level of focus and the source of our motivation. It's important to be thoughtful about what you agree to or decline, to protect your well-being. Look back at what you said yes or no to in the past few days. Were they the right decisions for your time and energy? Or do you now recognize something that drained you and didn't matter? Is there any joy you passed up because you took on too much in other areas?

4

GET BACK TO BASICS

Then he [Elijah] lay down under the bush and fell asleep.

All at once an angel touched him and said, "Get up and eat." He looked around, and there by his head was some bread baked over hot coals, and a jar of water. He ate and drank and then lay down again.

The angel of the Lord came back a second time and touched him and said, "Get up and eat, for the journey is too much for you." So he got up and ate and drank. Strengthened by that food, he traveled forty days and forty nights until he reached Horeb, the mountain of God.

—1 Kings 19:5–8 (NIV)

SOMETIMES, WE SACRIFICE OUR PHYSICAL WELLNESS to meet the demands of our to-do list. Then, where is our strength for the journey? If God is to work through us, we can't shortchange our bodies. Even the prophet Elijah was reminded of that fact! When our body is dysregulated, we are unable to emotionally connect with others, mentally focus, or actualize our goals and dreams. Some ways out of that dysregulation can be pretty basic: Sleep well, eat nutritiously, stay hydrated, rest, be safe, and address illness or pain. In what area do you need to recommit this week, and what are some simple first steps you can take?

Everybody's not going to understand where God has called you to go, but that is not an excuse for you not to go there.

—CECE WINANS

HONOR YOUR CALLING

SOCIETY CAN OFTEN MAKE SELF-CARE FEEL COMPLICATED, but at its core, a God-centered view of self-care is simply being good stewards of our lives. Have you ever thought of it that way? Throughout Scripture, Jesus demonstrated this principle. Let's reflect on one powerful example.

When it seemed like Jesus had arrived too late to save Lazarus—four days after his death—He was really right on time. Confident in His identity as the Son of God, Jesus knew His purpose: to glorify His Father and complete His mission of bringing salvation to humanity. Jesus understood He had the power to raise Lazarus from the dead, so arriving after Lazarus had already passed allowed room for a greater miracle—the resurrection. Jesus did not allow himself to become hastened by the expectations set by others or attempt to be in several places simultaneously. Instead, He honored His God-aligned priorities, staying true to His purpose and the timing set by His Father.

We often talk about following in the footsteps of Jesus, yet how often do we consider that part of His example includes purposeful self-care rooted in identity and calling? Jesus teaches us to be good stewards of our lives, grounded in God's will.

Think back to a time when you were pulled in different directions by competing priorities. How did that affect your care for yourself and your attention to God's purpose? You're not alone if you felt torn. The good news is we can always return to the foundation of our God-given identity and purpose to guide our self-care. It begins with getting reacquainted with the miracle God made—you.

1

WHO ARE YOU?

*"This is my beloved Son,
in whom I am well pleased."*

—Matthew 3:17b (KJV)

Jesus was fully aware of His identity as the Son of God, and it was through His love and commitment to His Father that He fulfilled His unique calling. You too are one of a kind—God intentionally created you with a specific purpose in mind. When you think about your own identity, what qualities make you different from others? How has God uniquely shaped you to reflect His creativity?

Choose three words you would use to describe yourself and note why those words come to mind.

1.

2.

3.

2

TREASURE HUNT

For where your treasure is,
there your heart will be also.

—Luke 12:34 (NIV)

Whether you're aware of it or not, you carry a treasure inside of you. Your heart holds everything that you find valuable, and the way you live your life reflects what you treasure most. Take some time to consider what you value. Use the questions on the next page to explore what's stored in your heart.

What do you think about first thing in the morning and before you go to bed at night?

Who or what do you get excited talking about? What do you find yourself discussing often?

What plans have you made for yourself for the next week, month, year?

3

DO IT ON PURPOSE

Whatever you do,
do it all for the glory of God.

—1 Corinthians 10:31b (NIV)

Sometimes, without realizing it, we set our priorities based on our daily habits and routines. Over time, we can become so focused on maintaining the pattern that we lose sight of whether those routines serve our God-given purpose. But as God's creation, we are called to live for His glory in all areas of life.

One way to glorify God is to live intentionally. This means being mindful of why we do what we do and aligning our actions with His will and purpose for our lives.

THIS WEEK, SET AN INTENTION FOR HOW YOU PLAN TO GLORIFY GOD in your morning routine. Be specific about how you will create space for Him in your daily rhythm. One simple but powerful idea: When you wake up in the morning, try inviting the Holy Spirit into your day to teach you and guide you in all of your ways.

Sabbath is a period of "trying on" God's promised completion. . . . Sabbath is the inviting of all creation to be still and imagine the coming of God.

—ANDREW ROOT

BE BLESSED BY SABBATH

WHY DO WE SO OFTEN CARRY GUILT rather than receive the gift when it comes to Sabbath? Keeping Sabbath is one of the blessings God gives in the Ten Commandments, designed to keep us safe and thriving in Him. So, if you feel anxious or guilty when slowing down and resting, understand that this feeling is *not* from our Good Father.

Even machines need rest to function properly, but we are so much more than machines. Rest is built into our natural rhythms as necessary self-care. When we are well rested and lead balanced lives, we can show up daily as our healthiest selves. Throughout the book of Exodus, God emphasizes the importance of Sabbath, deeming it so holy that a failure to rest was a choice that led to destruction. While this may seem extreme, it's not inaccurate. When we neglect ourselves to overbooked schedules and endless commitments, racing anxiously from one task to another, we give ourselves over to exhaustion and burnout. But choosing rest is an act of faith in God's provision. By saying yes to rest, for ourselves and those around us, we are saying yes to God's ways, promises, and love. Rest is more than just stopping work; it's about realigning with God. In rest, He sanctifies us, bringing healing to what's been worn down by life's demands. He draws us away from the noise and rush and into beautiful places, reorienting us to His goodness.

Stillness might feel uncomfortable at first, but rest doesn't mean doing nothing. It's about actively spending time with God—delighting in Him, worshipping, and meditating on His Word. The exercises in this unit will lead you into the blessings of rest in simple ways.

1

A PLAYLIST FOR REST

MUSIC IS A DIVINE BRIDGE, CONNECTING HEARTS to the Lord and bringing healing to the soul. (Just read some Psalms!) Through music, we can offer praise and find peace. Create a playlist of songs that imparts to your spirit a truth you can rest in: that you are a broken yet beautiful, blessed, beloved child of God.

2

SWEET, SWEET SONG

THE LORD WELCOMES US TO LIFT OUR OWN WORDS. Even if you are not musical, your Father longs to hear your voice (Song of Solomon 2:14). Write some words of prayer, then raise them in song. Try using the tune of a favorite hymn, praise song, or even a lullaby or chorus you learned as a child. What matters is your heart, not hitting all the right notes.

3

MOVE TOWARD PEACE

REMEMBER, REST DOESN'T HAVE TO BE ABOUT SITTING STILL. When the body retains trauma, movement can be powerful for healing. Release your inhibitions and dance to the Lord like David danced (2 Samuel 6:14)—to your playlist from page 34 or your own praise rhythms from your prayer on page 35. Listen to your body and let it lead you in creative worship. How does it feel to let go and allow yourself to rest in movement?

4

FOLLOW JESUS'S LEAD

OUR BODIES CALL OUT FOR PHYSICAL REST, and it's okay to take it. Jesus took naps (Luke 8:23) to refresh Himself before continuing His work. If He needed to nap, why do we think we don't?

Find a safe, peaceful place to take a nap—whether it's your bed, a cozy chair, or a blanket outside. Set a timer for twenty minutes to prevent oversleeping. Lie down on your back and place one hand on your heart and the other on your belly. Breathe so that your belly rises and falls as your chest remains still. Let your mind wander if it needs to, but then gently bring it back to focus on your breath. You may or may not fall asleep, but you will enter a deep state of relaxation. Choose a few words to describe how you feel afterward.

5

DELIGHTS OF THE DAY

"Keep the Sabbath day holy. Don't pursue your own interests on that day, but enjoy the Sabbath and speak of it with delight as the Lord's holy day."

—Isaiah 58:13a (NLT)

SOMETIMES, ALL IT TAKES TO "ENJOY THE SABBATH" is reminding ourselves how delightful it is to fill our hearts with the Lord. Think about Scripture or prayers that have brought you healing when you felt depleted and defeated.

Write the powerful words in a beautifully creative way below, then meditate on them.

Consider printing the words on a canvas, mug, T-shirt, or other visual reminder for yourself and as a gift to encourage others.

“But ask the animals,
and they will teach you . . .
or speak to the earth, and
it will teach you . . .”

—JOB 12:7A, 8A (NIV)

FIND RESTORATION IN NATURE

GOD'S LOVE STORY WITH US STARTS IN A GARDEN. We are told that we are designed to lovingly steward over His creation. So, it's only natural that engaging with nature has a holistic healing effect—we get fulfillment in mind, body, and spirit when we follow our calling and commitment to nature. And despite our efforts to build up earthly kingdoms with high-rises, God still surrounds us with opportunities—both big and small—to take in His creation and the feelings of refreshment it brings.

Think about it: Most of the parables Jesus used to illustrate spiritual truths were drawn from nature and delivered in natural settings—from fields to seas to mountains. Scripture also tells us that Jesus "left the house and went *out* to a solitary place to pray" and "went *out* as usual" to the Mount of Olives to pray (emphasis added). Profound encounters with God often took place in the open air, whether atop mountains or in the middle of the sea.

When we look closely at Scripture, we see how God uses elements of the natural world—sea, dirt, animals, fire, rain, and trees—to sanctify and heal. We may think, "That was then, this is now," but modern research backs up scriptural wisdom. Time spent in nature contributes to better sleep, lower blood pressure, less stress, and reduced risk of chronic disease. In the hands of our great God, nature becomes a tool for divine intervention and soul-stirring self-care. The exercises in this unit will help you see God's restorative gifts reaching out to you through nature.

1

TAKE IT OUTSIDE

GOD CREATED US TO ENJOY AND FLOURISH IN NATURE. Yet, most of us spend the majority of our time indoors—at home, working, shopping, worshipping, dining, and even exercising at the gym. Make a list of activities that you can take outdoors this week. These could be as simple as enjoying your morning coffee outside, taking a phone call on a walk, or even tweezing your eyebrows in natural sunlight. Get creative!

2

NATURE'S CALM CLOSE

FOR THOSE TIMES WHEN YOU CAN'T GET OUTSIDE, choose a photo of nature that brings you peace—something you can turn to throughout your day. It could be a photo you took or one you simply appreciate. Make it your phone's or laptop's wallpaper, or place it somewhere you'll see often. What image did you choose, and how does it speak to you?

3

PAMPER YOUR SENSES

In just a few minutes, you can practice mindfulness by engaging your senses with nature. Step outside wherever and whenever you can, letting yourself notice the beauty around you that is often overlooked in the rush of daily life. Inspiration to get started:

+ Look at something in nature as though you're seeing it for the first time in your life.
+ Listen to the layers of sound around you, near and far.
+ Feel the wind, sun, or humidity on your skin. Smell the air.
+ Go barefoot for a moment and enjoy the texture of the ground beneath your feet.

HOW DO YOU FEEL AFTER TUNING IN TO NATURE'S RHYTHMS? What words describe your "before" and "after" state of mind, body, and soul?

Before	After

4

THE GIFT OF NURTURE

YOU DON'T NEED A GREEN THUMB to find pleasure and purpose in gardening. Start with one easy-to-care-for plant and check on it daily, meeting its needs—from water and pruning to words of affirmation and gratitude for being so beautiful (yep, we all need those!). If you live in the city, a potted plant by the window will do just fine. Caring for a plant reminds us that simply existing—and letting others care for us—is valuable. Read that last sentence again slowly; underline it; *take it to heart.*

As you tend to your plant, note how it's uniquely created with distinct care needs. What unique needs would be on *your* care tag? Whom can you share these needs with so they can support you?

5

LOOK TO THE CLOUDS

EACH DAY, THE SKY PRESENTS A DIFFERENT SCENE, and yet we can still appreciate its beauty. As you sketch the clouds today, reflect on how each day is a new gift from God, even when it doesn't look like what you expected.

To every thing there is a
season, and a time to every
purpose under the heaven:
A time to get, and a time
to lose; a time to keep, and
a time to cast away . . .

—ECCLESIASTES 3:1, 6 (KJV)

EMBRACE FREEDOM IN RELEASE

RELEASE IS SOMEWHAT SIMPLE TO DEFINE: setting something free, unbinding, letting go. So why does it seem so much more difficult to practice? Often, out of fear and insecurity, we hold on tightly—with a clenched fist or anxious grip. We think this will keep us safe, but it usually does the opposite. The more we cling, the more powerless we feel, and what we hold on to begins to weigh us down. It's exhausting to carry what we're meant to release.

We all have things in our lives that need to be let go—dreams, relationships, expectations, and even our own thoughts. They are keeping us from the better gifts God wants to offer us. Scripture shows us repeatedly that blessings await those who are willing to release and surrender. The Samaritan woman at the well released and surrendered her shame and cynicism to Jesus and ran back to her community, bursting with joy to share the Good News (John 4:4–42). On the other hand, the rich young man who was asked by Jesus to release and surrender his fortunes that enslaved him walked away sad and burdened by the weight of his possessions (Matthew 19:16–30, Mark 10:17–31, Luke 18:18–30).

If you feel like doubt blocks you, know you're not alone. It's an everyday choice to reach for God and release everything else that doesn't matter (or leads us down destructive paths). Letting go and leaning into the Lord might feel a little like free-falling at first, but trust will lead you to freedom and joy that propel you to move forward in a healthier direction. Releasing frees up your hands to claim what is better and your heart to receive what is healing.

1

OPEN YOUR HANDS

IN THE SPACE BELOW AND ON THE NEXT PAGE, or on separate sheets of paper, trace or draw an outline of your hands. Write "Keeping" above the first outline and "Releasing" above the second. Think about the people, places, ideas, habits, and things that contribute to your growth, maturity, purpose, and fulfillment. Add them in words, drawings, or collage-style cutouts inside your Keeping hand.

TURN YOUR THOUGHTS to people, places, ideas, habits, and things that can be destructive, hinder your God-centered goals, or limit your potential. Add them in words, drawings, or collage-style cutouts inside your Releasing hand. Ask God to help you follow through with what to hold tight and what to release.

2

OPEN YOUR HEART

USING YOUR RELEASING HAND (FROM PAGE 51) AS A GUIDE, choose one area of your life where you feel most weighed down by something you're holding on to—maybe it's a relationship, expectation, or fear. Write a spill-your-heart prayer, asking God to help you release it (and all the heaviness surrounding it) and make room for God's better gifts.

3

FEEL LIGHTER WITH A LETTER

THINK OF SOMEONE IN YOUR LIFE you haven't forgiven or a situation in which bitterness still lingers. Write a letter (you don't have to send it) to this person, expressing the hurt but also your desire to release both of you from the weight of unforgiveness.

4

CLEAR PHYSICAL CLUTTER

YOU DESERVE BEAUTY AND HARMONY in the spaces where you spend your time. Clearing clutter, mess, and noise around us can bring inner peace, rest, and quiet. But sometimes, our environment is so far from what we need it to be for rest and function that we become overwhelmed and stuck in the muck. What little space can you tackle in just fifteen to thirty minutes to bring more calm to your environment? Make a simple plan.

Focus space: ______________________________

Add	Take away	Freshen up

5

CLEAR EMOTIONAL CLUTTER

SOME PHYSICAL CLUTTER IS EASY TO LET GO OF, but other possessions can be harder to release when they're tied to deep-seated emotions. Is there something you're holding on to—like an unfinished project that weighs on you or a reminder of a past that no longer reflects who you are? Identify it here, and then take action: Place it in the trash, recycling, or donate pile.

Blessed are the curious, for they shall have adventures.

—LOVELLE DRACHMAN

HOLD SPACE FOR DISCOVERY

WHERE DID THE DAYS OF WONDERING AND WANDERING GO?
As adults, we often feel the pressure to have it all figured out—to plan every step from "Point A to Point B" and know all the answers, even down to what's for dinner each night. Playdates and recess are long gone, and it seems like asking "why?" too often is no longer acceptable. But that's not God's way. He invites us to embrace the holy curiosity He placed within us. He calls us to have childlike faith, always looking to Him for new lessons, connections, blessings, and mercies as we seek His Kingdom.

Jesus showed us the importance of childlike faith when He called a little child to Him (Matthew 18:3 NIV), saying to His disciples: "Truly I tell you, unless you change and become like little children, you will never enter the kingdom of heaven."

In the same way, Jesus invites us to come close and experience Him—not from a distance, but hands-on, with an open heart. Just like the woman who reached out to touch the hem of His garment in faith (Matthew 9:20–22, Luke 8:42b–48), we too can draw near to Jesus when we let go of our tightly controlled schedules and reach for Him. When we give ourselves space to seek Jesus, we find glimpses of the Kingdom of Heaven sprinkled throughout our days and waiting to be discovered.

In this unit, give yourself permission to wonder and wander. Ask the Holy Spirit to guide you to new places. Be curious about creation and the people around you, who are as wonderfully and fearfully made as you are. Look for the ways, both big and small, in which God is blessing you each day. Be like a child, eager to reach out and taste all the flavors of life's ice cream.

1

STEP INTO CURIOSITY

Think of a place, either physical or intellectual, that you've wanted to explore but keep putting off. It might be a local nature trail or a topic you've always wanted to learn about. Describe it below, making a plan to take your first steps into this new space.

What fears or excuses might be holding you back? Release them here.

Record your experience—in words or photography. If you choose words, consider writing a prayer of gratitude. If you choose to take photos, try a fresh perspective—look for new angles to reflect your growth and discoveries.

2

CONNECT THROUGH QUESTIONS

IT'S EASY TO GLIDE THROUGH OUR DAYS with simple "Hi, how are you?" and "Good" exchanges. But deeper connections are life-giving.

Invite an important person in your life to share more about their life and experiences. Let them open up as much as they are comfortable. What do you learn about them? What do you learn about yourself in the invitation and time spent together?

3

NO NEED TO KNOW IT ALL

NO MATTER HOW HARD WE TRY, we can't have all the answers and paths forward. But we don't need to. God places people in our lives who are meant to share His wisdom or lighten our burdens. Think about the people in your life who may offer valuable insights. Write down their names, and next to each, jot down a question or topic you could ask them about. Seeking help is a strength, not a weakness.

Name	Ask

4

A TASTE OF ADVENTURE

Life must be lived and curiosity kept alive.

—Eleanor Roosevelt

EVERY REVELATION THAT COMES OUT OF CURIOSITY doesn't need to be life-altering. Some discoveries can simply bring the joy that God wants us to have in this life. One great place to start: Try a new food. If you're not very taste-adventurous, explore a new flavor of ice cream, tea, or coffee, then build your way up to dishes you need to learn how to pronounce.

What do you try? How does it feel to take each bite or sip mindfully? Is there anything you learn about the history or culture of the food?

I praise you because I am fearfully and wonderfully made . . .

—PSALM 139:14 (NIV)

APPRECIATE YOUR BODY

HOW INCREDIBLE IT IS THAT OUR BODIES were crafted by God from the dust of the earth! The human body, in all its complexity, continues to amaze scientists and spark new discoveries. More importantly, our bodies are a divine masterpiece—sacred in God's sight. Taking care of this masterpiece is not a form of pampering; it's an act of praise and gratitude for the incredible gift God has given us.

When we see our bodies as God's creation, our motivation shifts. We understand that caring for our bodies is an essential part of honoring God's work. When we nurture our bodies, we're nurturing the temple where God's Spirit dwells. Learning to appreciate and value our bodies as sacred can inspire us to adopt healthier habits and make better choices.

Just like an astronaut's suit allows them to experience and navigate outer space, our bodies allow us to interact with the physical world. They protect us, nourish us, and help us live out the life God has planned for us. One day, we will receive incorruptible bodies, free from decay, but until then, our responsibility is to care for the one we've been given.

Embracing body appreciation is about seeing yourself as God sees you—a work of art worth cherishing. Developing healthy habits and a lifestyle of self-care is not just about longevity but about living in gratitude for the miracle of your body every day.

1

THE HOUSE-SITTING VIEW

Do you not know that your bodies are temples of the Holy Spirit, who is in you, whom you have received from God? You are not your own; you were bought at a price. Therefore honor God with your bodies.

—1 Corinthians 6:19–20 (NIV)

WE DON'T OWN OUR BODIES; they belong to God, Who created us and breathed life into us. If we believe we will someday need to give an account of how we've cared for the bodies He entrusted to us, it's important to take this responsibility seriously. Imagine someone asked you to house-sit while they're away on a long journey. How would you care for their home, ensuring it's in good condition upon their return? The same thoughtfulness applies to caring for your body. How can this perspective change the way you approach stewardship of the body God has given you?

JUST LIKE WITH HOME REPAIRS AND MAINTENANCE, it's better to be proactive than reactive regarding health. List any doctor visits or screenings you've been meaning to schedule. Commit to making the needed appointments this week.

2

CELEBRATE GOD'S MASTERPIECE

What is it you want to change? Your hair, your face, your body? Why? For God is in love with all those things and he might weep when they are gone.

—St. Catherine of Siena

WE CAN WAX POETIC ABOUT THE BEAUTY of the ocean, mountains, sunrises, and sunsets all day long. But our physical bodies (every part!) are God's amazing creations too. Choose one part of your body you tend to be hard on—whether it's your prominent nose, achy knees, or soft belly—and consider it through God's eyes.

Express specific gratitude for the part you have chosen. ("Thank you, belly, for housing and protecting the most important internal body parts responsible for healthy functioning.") Then identify at least one small act you can offer to recognize and bless that part of your body. (Examples: Rub your belly each night with massage oil or lotion; inhale and exhale deeply, feeling your belly rise and fall; learn belly dancing.)

Words of Gratitude

Acts of Compassion

3

LISTEN FROM HEAD TO TOE

GOD GAVE THE BODY LANGUAGE to provide us with important information. Doctors can check our body temperature, heart rhythms, markers in our blood, and many other measures. Those aches and pains you feel are calls for attention. But our bodies' cries can get drowned out if we don't prioritize and practice listening. To build awareness, try a body scan:

+ Get into a comfortable position, either sitting or lying down.
+ Begin by taking some deep breaths.
+ As you continue breathing, focus on one body part or area at a time, starting at your toes. Pay attention to any sensations. Do you feel any tingling, numbness, pressure, tightness, or discomfort?
+ Repeat this as you work your way up through your feet, ankles, calves, knees, thighs, torso, shoulders, neck, and head.

What messages did your body send you? For example, where do you feel your body holding stress?

WORKING UP YOUR BODY, go back and tighten any tense areas muscle by muscle as you breathe deeply. Slowly release each body part as you release your breath. Ask for a blessing on that body part before moving on to other areas as needed. This progressive relaxation exercise works well as part of a bedtime routine for a better night's sleep.

Through him all things were made; without him nothing was made that has been made.

—JOHN 1:3 (NIV)

TAP INTO CREATIVITY

CREATIVITY IS A BEAUTIFUL EXPRESSION of our God-given gifts and a powerful form of Christian self-care. In the very first chapter of Genesis, we see God as the ultimate Creator, shaping the world and all that's in it. Made in His image, we are invited to partake in that creative process—not just through art or crafts, but in how we solve problems, approach life, and express ourselves. Engaging in creativity is more than a hobby; it's a way to connect with God, reflect His nature, and nurture our souls.

In a world that often pushes productivity and perfection, creativity allows us to pause, step outside those pressures, and embrace the freedom to express who we are in Christ. Through creativity, we can quiet the noise of life, experience joy, and explore the gifts God has placed within us. Whether it's through writing, painting, gardening, or even cooking, these moments of creative expression can become acts of worship, helping us to restore balance and care for ourselves spiritually, emotionally, and mentally.

Creativity helps us release burdens, explore new perspectives, and ultimately draw closer to God. It's an opportunity to rest in His presence, knowing that we don't need to strive for perfection—He already loves us just as we are. By engaging in creativity, we can nurture our minds and hearts while embracing the joy of God's creativity at work in us.

1

CREATE A VISUAL PRAYER

Instead of coming to God with words, try using visuals. Draw, paint, or collage images that represent your prayers, thoughts, and reflections. Let your creativity flow (on the next page or separate paper) without worrying about how it looks. Consider how this creative process opens new pathways for communication with Him.

2

LETTER GOD'S LOVE

Choose a Bible verse that speaks to you and hand-letter it below in anything from bubble letters to calligraphy. As you put pen to paper, think about how the process allows the Scripture to take root in your heart and mind. How does it deepen your connection with God's Word?

3

TRADE YOUR GIFTS

God has gifted us all differently. What creative expression can you share with someone else—whether through a gift you make for them or a skill you teach them?

Who is gifted in a way that you admire? What could you ask them to make for you or teach you?

4

WALK IN CREATION

God spoke today in flowers, and I, who was waiting on words, almost missed the conversation.

—Ingrid Goff-Maidoff

TAKE A WALK OUTSIDE AND GATHER NATURAL ITEMS like leaves, stones, or flowers. When you return, use these items to create something—a simple arrangement, a nature mandala, or a small craft. As you create, think about how God's creativity is reflected in nature and in you.

What did you make? How did this simple act of creativity remind you of His presence and care?

We are all different but we depend on each other.

—ROMANS 12:5 (NLV)

CONNECT WITH YOUR PEOPLE

GOD'S DESIGN FOR COMMUNITY IS EVIDENT from the beginning. He created Eve to be by Adam's side because it wasn't good for him to be alone. God instructed them to be fruitful and build a family, showing His desire for us to live in relationship with others. Jesus also emphasized community by gathering disciples and working closely with them. As part of the Holy Trinity, He understood the value of connection.

Yet today, many of us face a loneliness crisis. We often spend much of our time isolated in our homes, cars, screens, and individual routines. Whether we're working remotely, balancing busy schedules, scrolling through social media, or simply feeling too tired at the end of the day, it's easy to withdraw from real-life connections. While it's important to have moments of solitude, too much isolation can leave us feeling disconnected from others and God.

Sometimes, past hurts or painful experiences can also hold us back, causing us to protect ourselves in ways that make genuine connection difficult. If that resonates with you, seeking help from a trained professional can be a valuable step toward healing and reclaiming the ability to connect.

No matter where you are today, God is ready to lead you into a healthy, caring community where you can thrive. His desire is for us to experience self-care that overflows into caring for others, creating expanding circles of connection. It starts with small, intentional steps toward engaging with the people around us and opening ourselves to community. The exercises in this unit are designed to help you build and nurture those communities of support.

1

TRUST YOUR PEOPLE METER

HAVE YOU EVER NOTICED THAT SOME PEOPLE LEAVE YOU FEELING ENERGIZED while others leave you depleted? Increasing your awareness of how you are affected by your interactions is good self-care. Who makes you feel safe, alive, and energized? How can you spend more time with them?

WHO DO YOU NEED TO LIMIT INTERACTIONS WITH?

How can you protect and conserve your energy when you're with them? (Examples: Set hard stops—have someone break up the meeting. Or bring along an ally.) Avoid interactions with anyone who makes you feel unsafe or has harmed you in the past.

2

CHOOSE YOUR INNER CIRCLE

WE CAN LEARN FROM JESUS'S EXAMPLE and choose an inner circle of people we can trust. Surround yourself with people who share your convictions, accept you, and care for you well. Depending on your lifestyle, you may need multiple inner circles in each space that you occupy. For example, you may have a few friends from high school or college that you keep in touch with and one or two coworkers you hang out with at work and sometimes after hours. These then would represent two separate inner circles, depending upon how you choose to engage with each group.

Take a moment to draw the circles in your life, then jot down the names of people you can trust inside the circles.

3

PARTNER IN PRAYER

REACH OUT TO SOMEONE YOU CAN CONNECT WITH regularly as a prayer partner. (Not sure where to start? Ask a leader in your faith community for help.) Set times for scheduled check-ins, then simply invite the Holy Spirit to lead you in prayer for each other. Take turns praying over every area of your lives—your family, your health, your finances, your work, your community, your nation. Pray about any challenges or sources of stress. Pray about your relationship with God. Confess where you are lacking and ask God to help you specifically in those areas.

My prayer partner:

When and where we will meet:

Best way to contact for emergency sessions:

Some specific ongoing prayer requests for each other:

4

TOGETHER AT A TABLE

INVITE SOMEONE (or a couple or a group) you haven't seen in a while to join you for coffee or a meal. Sharing food has significant spiritual meaning and can play a role in bonding and strengthening human connections. Try to be present at the table. Feel free to take a photo to share below and in a note of gratitude to your friend(s) later, but resist the urge to post pics online. Savor the in-person experience. How do you feel after the meetup?

5

GROUP GRATITUDE

WHETHER YOU BELONG TO A BOOK CLUB, sports league, recovery group, or volunteer team, being part of a bigger circle can bring you a sense of cooperation, new connections, and camaraderie.

What groups are you a member of now that give you that sense of support and belonging? List them below and thank God for them.

What new groups might you consider joining?

"Ask and it will be given to you; seek and you will find; knock and the door will be opened to you."

—MATTHEW 7:7 (NIV)

ASK FOR WHAT YOU NEED

BABIES TELL US WHAT THEY NEED through their nonverbal and verbal communication—and they don't give up until their needs are met. As we grow, we tend to think people are mind readers. Sometimes pride gets in the way, and we can become more reluctant to assertively request what we need for fear of rejection, dismissal, disapproval, or appearing incompetent or lazy. But self-reliance isn't God's design.

When we push through every day with a consistent sense of self-sufficiency, we deprive ourselves of the blessing of collaborating with God and others to live life more efficiently, effectively, and abundantly. James 4:2 (ESV) says, "You do not have, because you do not ask." Think of the missed opportunities when you could have asked someone for support or help instead of struggling all alone. Consider that you could have given the other person a chance to say yes to God and answer His calling with their gifts.

Just in case you're still not convinced, look to the Bible. From Genesis to Revelation, we see examples of Spirit-filled servants of God asking others for help or support: Moses leaning on Aaron, Jethro, and Joshua; David leaning on Jonathan; Esther and Mordecai leaning on each other to fulfill God's purpose; Barak leaning on Deborah; Ruth leaning on Naomi and Boaz; Paul leaning on Silas and Aquila and Priscilla; and even Jesus leaning on His disciples to distribute food, fetch a colt, and extend his Kingdom. God isn't just okay with us turning to others; He *wants* us to lean on Him and the people He has placed around us. This is His design—that we should care for each other according to the abilities He has blessed us with, give and take. It starts with honest asks.

1

TAKE TWO TO GOD

SIT IN QUIETNESS BEFORE GOD and think about an everyday area where you can invite Him in. What do you need that you have previously written off as too little or insignificant to bring to God? (Remember that God cares for the sparrow—Matthew 10:29–31.) Write out your prayer below.

NOW, BE BOLD AND ASK BIG. Watch how your faith increases and He responds to your requests that align with His will. He will exceed the expectations of those who ask in earnest. Ask for wisdom, insight, grace, open doors, healing . . . don't put limits on what God wants to do for you. He delights in those who cry out to Him and proves Himself mighty and capable to those who trust in Him for help. Cry out here.

2

TURN TO OTHERS

Carry each other's burdens, and in this way you will fulfill the law of Christ.

—Galatians 6:2 (NIV)

THINK ABOUT THE PEOPLE God has placed in your life. If you've been reluctant to ask for what you need in the past, it can help to start slowly communicating simpler needs to them and work up to bigger asks.

Create a ladder with some simpler requests at the bottom and tougher tasks at the top that you can ask of others in the next week. Some examples that may fall on different levels on the ladder depending on your assertiveness and relationship with the other person: temperature adjustment at home or in the car; help with household chores; a hug or listening ear; slower speech or repeated instructions; personal space or time alone; tutoring or instruction in a particular subject or task.

3

YOUR PREPAREDNESS PLAN

REMEMBER THOSE EMERGENCY CONTACTS ON SCHOOL FORMS? Make a list of your grown-up go-to contacts, noting what support they offer—maybe the best listening ear, a comforting meal, or a place to find some quiet, professional counseling. Remind yourself of your resources, and don't be afraid to call on them when the need arises.

Contact	Support

ENGAGING IN RELATIONSHIPS where giving is reciprocal is healthy. Offering ourselves and others chances to be blessed by giving and receiving is both protective and fulfilling. What do you feel God is calling you to bring to your relationships?

Where is He telling you that you're overextended and need to draw some limits? He wants you to shine bright, not burn out!

Silence is a sacred discipline, a grace of the Holy Spirit.

—HENRI NOUWEN

QUIET YOUR SOUL

WHERE DO WE GO IN THIS NOISY WORLD to find the peace that we so desperately crave? Simply, into the presence of God's love. Technically, we can do this anytime, anywhere—but it takes practice to connect with God in the hustle culture of our days. One of the best ways to start is by carving out moments of solitude and silence. Don't feel you need to escape to a remote retreat center to find this peace. Solitude isn't about isolation; it's about setting aside time to attune and attend to yourself within God's embrace. It's about detaching from the distractions of the world and drawing closer to God in a deeper, more intimate way.

Similarly, silence isn't about finding the perfect quiet environment but about shifting your focus. It's choosing to turn your attention away from the noise—both external and internal—and listen for the small, still voice of God. This voice brings *shalom*, which means wholeness, wellness, peace, and satisfaction for your soul.

Your goal is to hear God's voice above all others, allowing it to affirm your identity and worth. When you have this strong foundation, the opinions and expectations of others no longer control you. Learning to be still and finding your peace requires practice, so begin with short moments of solitude and silence. Gradually, work your way up to longer periods as you grow in your ability to center yourself in God's presence.

1

THE SCROLL BREAK

SOME OF THE NOISE IN OUR LIVES COMES FROM OUR SCREENS. Try scheduling a complete fast from social media this week—or at least set some screen time limits. Notice your thoughts, mood, and energy when you are quiet and not engaging with social media. Are you more attentive and mindful? Are you more content with yourself and your life? Are you more connected with your people and your environment?

If the FOMO feels tough to handle, who can you reach out to one-on-one (and in person, if possible) to give you a connected feeling? How can you support each other in healthier online habits?

2

GIVE YOURSELF FIVE

TRADE YOUR ANXIETY FOR MINDFUL PUNCTUALITY. Wherever you need to go in the next few days, plan to arrive at your destination five minutes early. Don't look for a way to be "productive" in those moments; instead, just close your eyes and seek stillness. What words of prayer can you connect with (your own or a traditional prayer) that will send peace and blessing before you and take gratitude with you before you exit your car?

3

SPACE IN THE DAY

WAKE UP HALF AN HOUR EARLIER or head to bed half an hour later than everyone else in your home. Use the time to do something relaxing or inspiring—write in a journal, follow a guided meditation, pray, read, pamper a pet, or savor the sensory pleasures of your skin-care routine. Resist the temptation to make calls, text, watch TV, or even listen to podcasts—just be quiet. Engage in your activity mindfully, silently, and in solitude. What do you choose, and how does it feel?

4

HEAR HIS WORDS

ALLOW THE LORD TO COME INTO YOUR heart as you rest in Him. Choose to simply be still and listen or be led to any passage to which your Bible opens. Either way, write down the words of comfort, correction, and counsel you receive or sketch the message you sense.

Praise be to the God and Father of our LORD Jesus Christ, the Father of compassion and the God of all comfort.

—2 CORINTHIANS 1:3 (NIV)

WELCOME COMFORT

ALLOWING OURSELVES COMFORT—both physical and emotional—is a vital form of Christian self-care. In a fast-paced world that often celebrates hustle and self-denial, many of us feel guilty about seeking comfort, as if it's indulgent or selfish. Yet, God's Word encourages us to rest in Him and receive His comfort. Jesus invites us to come to Him when we are weary and burdened, promising to give us rest (Matthew 11:28). Comfort isn't about escaping life's challenges; it's about recognizing our human need for rest, renewal, and care—just as God designed.

Comfort can take many forms. Physically, it may mean getting adequate rest, nourishing your body with good food, or enjoying a warm, peaceful environment. Emotionally, it's allowing yourself to experience peace, grace, and gentleness when life becomes overwhelming. By embracing comfort as a gift from God, we honor our bodies and souls as temples of the Holy Spirit. This practice not only helps us heal and recharge but also deepens our connection with God, Who is often described as our ultimate Comforter.

Rather than viewing comfort as a weakness, we can see it as an opportunity to experience God's love in a tangible way. When we allow ourselves to be comforted, we practice trust in God's care, opening our hearts to His presence and restoration.

1

CORNER OF WARMTH

DEDICATE A CORNER OF YOUR HOME as a comfort space where you can rest in God's presence. Fill it with items that bring you peace—such as soft pillows, warm blankets, your Bible, and soothing scents. Sketch what you want the space to look like.

2

HOLD TIGHT TO TRUTH

PLACE A FEW BIBLE VERSES that offer comfort where you can see them regularly—on your mirror, in your comfort space, by your bed. Meditate on these verses often as you imagine that you are standing before God. Picture Him smiling with His arms wide open to give you a big hug. Hold this image in your mind as you stretch your arms and give yourself a hug, holding it for a few breaths. Physically, hugging releases the happy hormones, oxytocin and endorphins, which reduce stress and lift your spirits. Your warm embrace also sends messages of love and acceptance to your soul. What are some times you could use this comfort practice?

3

COMFORT FOOD WITH INTENTION

PREPARE (OR PURCHASE) A WHOLESOME MEAL that brings you comfort, but do so mindfully by reflecting on God as your provider. Before eating, say a prayer of thanks for the nourishment and comfort God gives. What do you make? How does your expression of gratitude enhance your experience?

4

HONEST CHECK-IN

DON'T BRUSH OFF YOUR EMOTIONS—WHATEVER THEY ARE. Find a healthy release—punch a pillow, let those tears flow. (Remember, John 11:35 doesn't say "Jesus powered through"; it says "Jesus wept.") Then write down what's been weighing on your heart and ask God to comfort you in these areas. Notice how letting go allows you to rest more fully in His comfort.

In peace I will lie down
and sleep,
for you alone, LORD,
make me dwell in safety.

—PSALM 4:8 (NIV)

SLEEP IN GOD'S PEACE

SLEEP IS ONE OF GOD'S GIFTS TO US, designed to refresh our bodies and minds so we can live fully and serve Him well. Even God rested after creating the world, showing us how important it is to take time to rest (Genesis 2:2–3). In Psalm 127:2, we are reminded that God grants sleep to those He loves, and Jesus invites the weary to come to Him for rest (Matthew 11:28). Yet, many of us struggle to prioritize sleep, letting stress, anxiety, or the demands of our schedules rob us of this vital need.

Lack of sleep affects more than just our energy levels. It messes with our focus, our emotions, and even our spiritual well-being. When we don't rest, we can't live out God's purpose for us as joyfully and fully as we should. Prioritizing restful sleep is an important part of self-care, honoring the bodies God has given us and allowing us to show up as our best selves in our daily lives.

This section will help you see sleep as an act of trusting God to take care of your needs. Through the exercises, you'll learn to create a peaceful environment, let go of stress, and prepare both your body and mind for deep, restorative rest.

1

PUT WORRIES TO BED

Unless the Lord watches over the city, the watchman stays awake in vain.

—Psalm 127:1b (ESV)

REFLECT ON AREAS WHERE WORRY OR ANXIETY may be keeping you awake—whether it's revisiting one small moment from the day or holding on to a bigger situation that's honestly out of your control. Write down your concerns and then release them to God, trusting Him to take care of them while you rest. Practice repeating a simple phrase, such as "I trust You, Lord," as you fall asleep, reminding yourself that God is in control.

Tonight, I am releasing . . .

Words I can repeat and rest in:

2

SIMPLE ROOM REDO

TAKE A MOMENT TO LOOK AROUND your bedroom. How does it make you feel? Is it a calm, peaceful place where you can truly rest? If not, don't worry—it's easy to fix! Make a quick list of small changes you can implement to create a more relaxing environment. Maybe you need to declutter a bit, adjust the temperature, or set a no-screens-before-bed rule. Whatever it is, jot it down, and then make it happen. You deserve a peaceful space where you can unwind and recharge at the end of the day.

3

DESIGN A ROUTINE

IT'S TEMPTING TO JUST CRASH AT THE END OF THE DAY, but creating a consistent bedtime routine can work wonders for your sleep. Think of activities that help you relax—like reading a calming Bible passage, journaling your thoughts, saying a prayer, or soaking in a warm bath. Write down what your ideal routine looks like and try sticking to it for a week. Your body will start recognizing these signals, and sleep will come much easier.

I did my best, and God did the rest.

—HATTIE MCDANIEL

TRUST GOD'S DREAMS

IN TODAY'S CULTURE, IT'S EASY TO GET CAUGHT UP in filling our schedules and homes, chasing social media likes, and measuring success by monetary gains. But when we base our self-worth on accomplishments or accumulation rather than our inherent value as God's beloved children, we experience a roller coaster of emotions—ranging from self-rejection and low self-esteem to pride and disdain for others. We exhaust ourselves chasing an illusion of perfection.

Remember this: God's love for us has never been, and never will be, based on our productivity or usefulness. He loves us simply because of who He is, as demonstrated through Jesus. Nothing we could ever do is enough to earn God's favor—and that's the beauty of it. His favor is freely received by faith, not through doing or earning, but through believing and receiving. Yet, we often resist this gift because we view receiving as a sign of weakness or dependency.

The truth is, God's dreams and plans for us are far better than anything we could imagine for ourselves. When we let go of the need for the three pesky P's (productivity, perfectionism, and people-pleasing), we open ourselves to His dreams for our lives—dreams rooted in His love, not our accomplishments. By trusting His plans, we can live with greater purpose, joy, and freedom, knowing our worth is secure in Him. Let go, and allow yourself to dream God's dreams for you.

1

ROOT OUT THE THREE P's

For each one, describe a situation where you've allowed the trap to control your actions or self-worth.

Productivity

____

____

____

Perfectionism

____

____

____

People-pleasing

____

____

____

WRITE ABOUT ONE AREA OF YOUR LIFE where you'll focus more on receiving God's love and plans for you instead of striving on your own. Ask God to bless your efforts.

2

PICTURE HIS PLANS

"For I know the plans I have for you," declares the Lord, "plans to prosper you and not to harm you, plans to give you hope and a future."

—Jeremiah 29:11 (NIV)

SIT IN A QUIET SPACE AND ASK GOD to show you what His dreams and plans are for your life—or even just the next few weeks, to get started. Write down any thoughts, images, or Scriptures that come to mind. Consider what steps you can take to align with His vision instead of your own.

Create a visual representation of God's dreams for you—this could be through drawing or collage (often called a "vision board"). Keep this in a place you'll see often as a reminder to trust His beautiful plans.

3

COURAGE FOR YOUR OWN PATH

GOD HAS TAKEN GREAT CARE TO DESIGN and form each of us into unique individuals with a specific purpose. So, how do we begin to walk away from others' expectations without fear?

Remember when we were kids and dared each other to do the unexpected? Once a week, do one little (even silly) thing that places you in a rebellious position to the expectations and opinions of others. Examples: Wear sequins to the grocery store, sing in a public place, eat with your fingers when you're out with friends. Once your comfort level increases, you can apply the principle to more serious and sensitive things, like transparently sharing how you feel or think with others instead of passively agreeing to avoid rejection.

What are three small acts of rebellion you can try this week?

1. ______________________________

2. ______________________________

3. ______________________________

Report back after you carry out your plans. How does it feel when you start? Does it get easier?

____

____

____

____

____

____

A joyful heart is good medicine . . .

—PROVERBS 17:22A (ESV)

SEEK AND CELEBRATE JOY

JOY IS A PRECIOUS GIFT FROM GOD, deeply rooted in His love and faithfulness. Amid our daily challenges, it's easy to overlook the simple blessings that fill our lives. Yet, joy isn't just a natural response to God's goodness—it's also a way of caring for our souls. The Bible repeatedly calls us to rejoice, give thanks, and celebrate, reminding us that joy reflects God's presence in our lives (Philippians 4:4).

Christian joy goes beyond fleeting emotions or external circumstances. It's grounded in the deep, unshakable assurance of God's love and grace. By choosing to seek joy intentionally, we honor the life God has given us, recognizing that even in hardship, His goodness remains steadfast. Taking time to celebrate helps us pause, reflect, and appreciate the beauty and blessings all around us, keeping our hearts anchored in God's faithfulness.

When we make space for joy, we invite refreshment, hope, and renewal into our lives. Celebrating God's gifts—both big and small—nurtures our spirit and helps us stay connected to His unwavering love. Embracing joy as an act of self-care is a powerful way to reflect God's love for us, and you'll explore this more through the exercises in this unit.

1

GATHER THE GOOD

EACH DAY THIS WEEK, WRITE DOWN THREE THINGS that bring you joy, no matter how small. Thank God for these blessings, and notice how your outlook and energy change.

Sunday

1. ______________________________

2. ______________________________

3. ______________________________

Monday

1. ______________________________

2. ______________________________

3. ______________________________

Tuesday

1. ______________________________

2. ______________________________

3. ______________________________

Wednesday

1. ______________________________
2. ______________________________
3. ______________________________

Thursday

1. ______________________________
2. ______________________________
3. ______________________________

Friday

1. ______________________________
2. ______________________________
3. ______________________________

Saturday

1. ______________________________
2. ______________________________
3. ______________________________

You can keep the practice going with a "Joy Jar," where you place notes of joyful moments and reflect on them at the end of the month.

2

SMALL VICTORY PARTY

IDENTIFY A SMALL ACCOMPLISHMENT FROM YOUR WEEK—whether it's completing a task or making time for rest—and celebrate it in a fun way. Buy yourself a cupcake and put a candle on top. Make a silly certificate that salutes your achievement. Dance around to a victory song. What's the plan? Describe the celebration in words or post a photo below.

3

LIVE WITH LAUGHTER

GOD DESIGNED SOMETHING WONDERFUL in laughter. It boosts your mood and immunity while decreasing stress levels and easing pain. What makes you laugh? Make a list below that you can turn to anytime you need it.

Person ______________________________

Movie/show ______________________________

Book ______________________________

Blog/podcast ______________________________

Photo ______________________________

Memory ______________________________

____

4

HEADLINES WITH HEART

When we seek to discover
the best in others,
we somehow bring out
the best in ourselves.

—William Arthur Ward

WE ALL KNOW THE NEWS CAN GET OVERWHELMING. But staying connected to uplifting stories can help push back against the negativity. Watch for stories that spark joy by highlighting faith, strength, courage, beauty, or acts of kindness.

Jot down or create a collage of their headlines. Use these as little reminders that there's still so much good out there, and keep your focus on what's possible.

Let us then approach God's throne of grace with confidence, so that we may receive mercy and find grace to help us in our time of need.

—HEBREWS 4:16 (NIV)

GIVE YOURSELF GRACE

FOR MANY OF US, OFFERING GRACE TO OTHERS FEELS SO MUCH EASIER than offering it to ourselves. We all have moments when we fall short—whether of our own expectations or others'. When this happens, it's easy to slip into self-criticism, especially when those expectations were unrealistic to begin with. Too often, we hold ourselves to impossible standards, setting ourselves up for disappointment. This can lead to a cycle of harsh self-judgment that's hard to break.

But God calls us to something different. Instead of being hard on yourself, try offering the same grace you'd extend to a close friend. If a friend came to you feeling discouraged, you'd likely comfort them, remind them of their worth, and offer compassion. You deserve that same kindness. Remember, perfection is an illusion—we're not meant to achieve it. We were created to be whole in relationship with God, not through our own efforts. In those moments when your flaws feel overwhelming, take heart—God sees you, loves you, and cherishes you exactly as you are.

God's love for you is unconditional and unwavering, and He invites you to accept that same love for yourself. Grace is one of God's greatest gifts, and it's meant to be applied to your own heart, too. Remind yourself that you are enough—not because you are perfect, but because God's love is perfect. Embracing His grace frees you from the weight of unrealistic expectations, allowing you to rest in the truth of who you are in Him. The reflections in this unit are designed to help you see we all fall short (Romans 2:23) and are only complete in God.

1

TRUST THE TRANSFORMATION

THINK OF RAW MATERIALS LIKE UNREFINED GOLD, a pearl within an oyster, or paint within a tube—plain until touched by masterful hands. Now, imagine yourself as raw material. In what areas are you trying by your own (exhausting!) effort to develop yourself instead of trusting God, the Master Creator, to shape you into His masterpiece?

2

BEAUTY IN IMPERFECTION

BUILDING A HEALTHY RELATIONSHIP WITH imperfection is important. After all, it's part of life and humanity. At times, it connects us to other people who may be able to fill in gaps. In other situations, it reminds us that only Jesus can fill in our gaps. Consider all the imperfect parts of your life—you might think about your body, home, car, relationships, church, job, and neighborhood. What blessings have emerged from even the imperfect?

3

CHANGE THE NARRATIVE

And we know that in all things God works for the good of those who love him, who have been called according to his purpose.

—Romans 8:28 (NIV)

WE ARE NOT DEFINED BY WHAT HAPPENS TO US in life, but by how we trust God to bring us through to a victorious ending. Write about a painful experience you've survived or overcome, thanks to God's grace. Consider how you'd like to see yourself grow in the future. What can you change, and where do you need to trust God with what's beyond your control? Offer your story in gratitude and activate your faith in God's power to honor your prayers and heart's desires.

4

WE ARE NOT SAVIORS

Do small things with great love.

—Mother Teresa

WE CARE. WE GIVE. WE LOVE. But although we often expend a lot of energy trying, we cannot save. Only God can do that—through Jesus.

What "savior mission" in your life can you turn over to God as an act of confidence in Him and care for yourself?

5

PRAY TO OUR PEACE

You will keep in perfect peace
all who trust in you,
all whose thoughts are fixed on you!

—Isaiah 26:3 (NLT)

WHENEVER YOU FEEL TEMPTED TO TAKE ON too much or like everything is spinning out of control, simply breathe in and out slowly and deeply and center your heart in the Lord. Consider praying this adaptation of The Praises of God from St. Francis of Assisi.

Lord God,
You alone are holy, you who work wonders!
You are strong. You are great,
You are the Most High, King of heaven and earth.

You are all goodness, the highest Good.
You are love. You are wisdom.
You are humility. You are patience.
You are rest. You are peace.

You are joy. You are our delight.
You are justice. You are moderation.
You are all our wealth and riches overflowing.

You are beauty. You are gentleness,
You are our shelter, our guardian, and our defender.
You are strength. You are refreshment.
You are our courage. You are our haven and hope.
You are our faith. You are our complete consolation.
You are our life everlasting, Merciful Savior!

Amen.

ABOUT THE AUTHORS

Teresa Pressley, LMFT, is a New Jersey–licensed marriage and family therapist with the Center for Christian Counseling and Relationship Development. She has dedicated much of her adult life to serving others.

With a BS in Bible and Christian Counseling from Cairn University and an MA in Marriage and Family Therapy from Liberty University, Teresa provides counseling for adolescents and adults, focusing on self-esteem, depression, anxiety, relationships, premarital counseling, grief, stress, and spiritual concerns. She is trained in Eye Movement, Desensitization, and Reprocessing (EMDR) and Emotional Focused Therapy (EFT) and has worked as a behavioral assistant with the New Jersey Department of Children and Families for Mobile Response.

Since coming to faith at nineteen, Teresa has sought to live by obedience to God's Word. She was licensed as a minister in 2001 and has served as an associate minister, worship leader, women's ministry facilitator, Bible study teacher, and presenter on spiritual growth, relationships, mental health, and wellness.

Self-care guides Teresa in balancing the demands of her personal life, ministry, and career. She cherishes her faith, family, and close-knit White City community in New Jersey. Married to Rev. David Pressley for more than thirty-five years, they have raised four children. Teresa enjoys singing, family time, travel, and Zumba.

Teriz Michael, LCSW, felt a calling to leave a successful teaching career to serve in the mental health field. She now practices psychotherapy at the Center for Christian Counseling and Relationship Development in New Jersey.

With a BFA from the School of Visual Arts in New York City and an MSW degree from Rutgers University, Teriz integrates creativity and biblical principles into holistic counseling. She has extensive training in cognitive behavioral therapy, dialectical behavioral therapy, and solution-focused therapy. Previously, she worked as an intensive outpatient therapist with young adults at Rutgers University Behavioral Health Care and as a youth therapist at Catholic Charities.

Recovering from a serious illness taught Teriz the value of self-care, prompting her to leave behind overscheduling and overachieving. She now focuses on pleasing Jesus, prioritizing rest, saying no without guilt, and living with childlike faith. Although Teriz has served in various roles within professional and church communities in New Jersey and Egypt, she takes the most pride in simply being a child of God.

Teriz immigrated from Cairo, Egypt, to the United States in 1987. She lives in Middlesex County, New Jersey, with her husband of over twenty years, George, and their children, Anastasia and Simon. Teriz enjoys Bible study, kayaking, reading, photography, painting, writing, gardening, and power naps.